Keys
to an
Amazing
Life

Everyday Wisdom for
Your Success

T0155171

Daniel Taddeo

Keys to an Amazing Life: Everyday Wisdom for Your Success

Published by HigherLife Development Services Inc.
PO Box 623307
Oviedo, Florida 32762
www.ahigherlife.com

Paperback ISBN: 978-1-951492-89-2
Ebook ISBN: 978-1-951492-10-6

10 9 8 7 6 5 4 3 2 1

Printed in the United States of America.

TABLE OF CONTENTS

Introduction 1

1. Godliness and Cultural Change 5

2. Right or Wrong 9

3. Getting Along 13

4. Friends 15

5. God's Business Cards 17

6. Fruit 19

7. Giving 21

8. Forgiving 23

9. The Lord's Prayer 25

10. Stress 29

11. Accountability 33

12. Anger 35

13. Attitude 37

14. Money 39

15. Busy People 41

16. Character 45

17. Children and School 49

18. Consequences 55

19. Death: Heaven or Hell? 59

20. Denominationalism 63

21. Diligence 67

22. Education 69

23. Journey 73

24. Living the Moment 75

25. Love 79

26. Marriage 81

27. Paradox 85

28. Prayer 87

29. Relationships 89

30. Success 91

31. Television 95

32. Present 97

33. Room 99

34. Truth 105

35. Identity 109

36. Worry 111

37. Jesus 115

38. Growing 117

39. Boom 119

40. Judging 121

41. Patience 123

42. Procrastination 125

43. Birth 127

44. Temptation 129

45. Truthfulness 131

46. Worldliness 133

47. Walking 135

48. Resurrection 137

Bibliography 139

INTRODUCTION

Although there are exceptions, most people agree that a universal code of ethics does exist. Any kind of order would be impossible unless all civilized people have a set of principles that determine responsible behavior. C.S. Lewis wrote, "We know that people find themselves under a moral law, which they did not make and cannot quite forget even when they try, and which they know they ought to obey."

Most agree that no society could survive without moral laws that spell out right and wrong conduct. The question then becomes: whose morality will be legislated? All laws intrude on the morality of someone. Are there moral principles and guidelines that have withstood the unfailing test of time? I believe the answer is yes, and the following pages will reveal this to the reader.

Keys to an Amazing Life is a unique collection of essays and "notable quotables." They focus on two approaches to living life—Godliness vs. worldliness. These essays share wisdom past and present to help individuals become the best they can be, to help make families stronger, and to help keep our country principled and going in a positive direction.

Godliness is determined by God's word, the Bible.

Biblical principles never change; they are the same "yesterday, today and forever" (Hebrews 13:8, NIV).

The answer to America's problems does not lie in more government spending, more laws, more police, or more jails. At best, these actions focus on putting out fires rather than preventing them. Our situation calls for a return to the Biblical moral values on which our nation was founded.

Worldliness is determined by secular culture. It is the opposite of Godliness; its beliefs and prevailing conventions are constantly changing. These conventions have been popular in the past, they remain popular in the present, and they will continue to be popular in the future. However, popularity doesn't make them right.

In our culture, we often discover too late that what we thought was right turns out to be wrong, and what we thought was wrong turns out to be right. The test for a right decision is this: does it adhere to Biblical principles?

Our real choice is between Godliness and worldliness because "no one can serve two masters" (Matthew 6:24, NIV).

It's like trying to go in two different directions at the same time; you end up going in circles and you never reach your destination. Each person is responsible for deciding which path to take and what choices to make. In the end, it behooves each

of us to keep in mind that "we reap what we sow."
It can't be any other way!

—Daniel Taddeo

CHAPTER 1

GODLINESS AND CULTURAL CHANGE

God's word speaks about godlessness in 2 Timothy 3:1-5 (NIV), "But mark this: There will be terrible times in the last days. People will be lovers of themselves, lovers of money, boastful, proud, abusive, disobedient to their parents, ungrateful, unholy, without love, unforgiving, slanderous, without self-control, brutal, not lovers of the good, treacherous, rash, and conceited, lovers of pleasure rather than lovers of God – having a form of Godliness but denying its power. Have nothing to do with such people."

Culture consists of certain characteristics that an individual or a group of people have in common, which then evolve into a way of life that becomes known as society or civilization. Many people are concerned about how far our society has drifted from the principles that founded and guided our nation for over 200 years.

Over a period of time, a culture might remain the same, improve or decline. Some of those changes could impact our society in a negative way; they include personal appearance, behavior, family, non-parental influence, school, and sexuality.

Personal Appearance: conformity, earring placement, indiscreet dress, makeup, dyed hair, tattoos.

Behavior: drug and alcohol abuse, immediate gratification, situational ethics, susceptibility to fads, vandalism, vulgar talk.

Family: less church attendance, disobedience, divorce, fatherlessness/single motherhood, lack of manners, obesity.

Non-parental Influence: Internet, peer pressure, sexting, smart phones, television, video games.

School: absentees, dropouts, lack of after-school supervision, low test scores, no moral instruction, and school violence.

Sexuality: homosexuality, pornography, promiscuous sex, same sex marriage, sexually transmitted diseases, unwanted pregnancy.

Each category above could generate a discussion in itself. Family, for example, is the very foundation upon which society rests. It is the first and often the only place where children are nurtured, loved and accepted for what they are in an environment where they can learn principles and values that will help equip them for adulthood. Children can sense when family comes first, and this realization will bring out the best in them. They thrive when parents exercise strong leadership, which tells them they are loved, making them more receptive to instruction and guidance. Children especially should be taught to think twice before following the crowd because Matthew 7:13-14 (NIV) says, "Wide is the gate and broad is the road that leads to destruction, and many enter through it. But small is the gate and narrow the road that leads to life and only a few find it."

In our culture, we often discover too late that what we thought was wrong turns out to be right. The test for a right decision is: does it adhere to Biblical truth? Though a particular choice may seem right at the time, if Biblical standards are ignored, eventually the foolishness of that choice will become evident with negative consequences that are sure to follow.

History is filled with examples of great civilizations that have come and gone. They all experienced moral decay from within. Historian Edward Gibbon (1737-94) listed five major causes for the decline and fall of the Roman Empire:

1. The rapid increase of divorce: the undermining of the dignity and sanctity of the home, which is the basis of human society.

2. Increasingly higher taxes and the spending of public money for free bread and circuses for the populace.

3. The mad craze for pleasure: every year sports become more exciting and more brutal.

4. The building of gigantic armaments when the real enemy was within, the decadence of the people.

5. The decay of religion: faith fading into mere form, losing touch with life and becoming less important to guide the people.

History does not document one civilization that survived without a dominating number of morally strong families. How would you rate the moral state of America today? Has our culture changed for the better—or the worse?

CHAPTER 2
RIGHT OR WRONG

No two words in any language world-wide generate more controversy than Right and Wrong. Living is a matter of making choices. Choices can't be avoided. Every choice a person makes has consequences. Right (good) choices have positive consequences and wrong (bad) choices have negative consequences, so one's course of action is very critical. After much thought, study, and prayer, I decided to go with God's word – the Bible. It is the same "yesterday, today, and forever."

Right is any thought, spoken word, or action that agrees with God's word, the Bible. Wrong is any thought, spoken word, or action that disagrees with God's word, the Bible. When in doubt as to which choice to make, we can ask ourselves what would most people do, and then consider doing the opposite.

The most famous Biblical passage that clearly defines right and wrong is known as the Ten Commandments. The commandments can be divided into two groups; the first four tell us how to love God, while the remaining six tell us how to love and enhance our relationship with one another.

The Ten Commandments serve as a compass for living life from a Biblical point of view. After learning how to love God, the next big challenge is to treat others the way you want them to treat you! Ideally; God first, others second, self third.

You shall have no other gods before me.

You shall not make for yourself an idol (self-made gods)

You shall not take the name of the Lord your God in vain.

Remember the sabbath day by keeping it holy.

Honor your father and your mother.

You shall not murder.

You shall not commit adultery.

You shall not steal.

You shall not give false testimony against your neighbor.

You shall not covet.

Another Bible passage to ponder is the following Parable of the Sower:

"A farmer was sowing grain in his fields. As he scattered the seed across the ground, some fell beside a path, and the birds came and ate it. And some fell on rocky soil, where there was little depth of earth; the plants sprang up quickly enough in the shallow soil; but the hot sun soon scorched them and they withered and died, for they had so little root. Other seeds fell among thorns, and the thorns choked out the tender blades. But some fell on good soil, and produced a crop that was thirty, sixty, and even a hundred times as much as he had planted. If you have ears, listen" (Matthew 13:3-9, TLB). My understanding of this parable is that only one out of four people does his or her best to live according to God's word. This will vary from person to person because only Jesus lived it 100 percent. We reap what we sow.

"God grant me the serenity to accept the things I cannot change, the courage to change the things I can, and the wisdom to know the difference."

Amen.

CHAPTER 3

GETTING ALONG

Before you say anything to anyone, ask yourself three things: (1) Is it true? (2) Is it kind? (3) Is it necessary?

Make promises sparingly and keep them faithfully.

Never miss the opportunity to compliment or to say something encouraging to someone.

Refuse to talk negatively about others; don't gossip and don't listen to gossip.

Have a forgiving view of people. Believe that most people are doing the best they can.

Refuse to talk negatively about others; don't gossip and don't listen to gossip.

Keep an open mind; discuss, but don't argue. At most, disagree without being disagreeable.

Forget about counting to ten. Count to 1,000 before doing or saying anything that could make matters worse.

Let your virtues speak for themselves.

If someone criticizes you, see if there is any truth to what they are saying; if so, make changes. If there is no truth to the criticisms, ignore them and live so that no one will believe the negative remarks.

Cultivate your sense of humor; laughter is the shortest distance between two people.

Do not seek so much to be consoled, as to console; do not seek so much to be understood, as to understand; do not seek so much to be loved, as to love.

CHAPTER 4
FRIENDS

Friends are special people whom we admire and hold in high esteem. They help us live better lives, and we all need them. To have friends we must first be one.

But there are some qualities we need to have to be friends, according to God's plan:

1. Love – "A new commandment I give to you, that you love one another" (John 13:34-35, NASB).

2. Friendliness – "The man who has friends must himself be friendly" (Proverbs 18:24, NKJV).

> Let each of you look out not only for his own interests, but also for the interests of others.

3. Consistency – "A friend loves at all times" (Proverbs 17:17, NIV).

4. Loyalty - "Do not forsake your own friend" (Proverbs 27:10, NASB).

5. Peacemaker – "Let us pursue the things which make for peace and the things by which one

may edify another" (Romans 14:19, NKJV).

6. Listener – "Let every man be swift to hear, slow to speak, slow to wrath" (James 1:19, NKJV).

7. Praise and Encouragement – "Rejoice with those who rejoice, and weep with those who weep" (Romans 12:15, NASB).

8. Sincerity – "Let each of you look out not only for his own interests, but also for the interests of others" (Philippians 2:4, NKJV).

9. Supportiveness – "As iron sharpens iron, so a man sharpens the countenance [approval] of his friends" (Proverbs 27:17, NKJV).

CHAPTER 5

GOD'S BUSINESS CARDS

"Love your neighbor as yourself" (Matthew 22:1, NASB).

"And what does the Lord require of you? To act justly, to love mercy and to walk humbly with your God" (Micah 6:8, NIV).

"But the fruit of the Spirit is love, joy, peace, longsuffering, kindness, goodness, faithfulness, gentleness, self-control. Against such there is no law" (Galatians 5:22, NKJV).

> Whatsoever things are just, true, pure, lovely, of good report; if there be any virtue, and if there are any praise, think on these things.

"Whatsoever things are just, whatsoever things are true, whatsoever things are pure, whatsoever things are lovely, whatsoever things are of good report; if there be any virtue, and if there be any praise, think on these things" (Philippians 4:8, KJV).

"For God so loved the world, that he gave his

only begotten son, that whatsoever believeth in him should not perish, but have everlasting life" (John 3:16, KJV).

"Train up a child in the way he should go; and when he is old, he will not depart from it" (Proverbs 22:6, NASB).

"Give, and it will be given to you...For with the same measure that you use, it will be measured back to you" (Luke 6:38, NASB).

Help make the world a better place by sharing this message with as many people as possible.

CHAPTER 6

FRUIT

Fruit is the product of whatever seeds are planted. Seeds of God's Holy Spirit are belief, faith, and trust. They produce the necessary nourishment for living a meaningful life.

They are recorded in Galatians 5:22:

Love...A deep and spiritual experience

Peace...An undisturbed state of mind when God is in control

Patience...A willingness to wait without complaining

Kindness...Wanting the best for others

Goodness...Doing what is beneficial

> Love the Lord your God with all your heart and with all your soul and with all your mind and with all your strength.

Faithfulness...Believing in the unseen such as faith in God

Self-Control...Resisting what's wrong and doing what's right

To all those who truly try (to the best of their ability to live by these principles), progress is sure

19

to follow!

God summarizes the whole Bible with the greatest commandment in Mark 12:30-31 (NIV):

"'Love the Lord your God with all your heart and with all your soul and with all your mind and with all your strength.' The second is this: Love your neighbor as yourself.'"

CHAPTER 7

GIVING

Giving is something that doesn't come easily to most people. Human nature leans much more toward receiving than giving. This attitude changes only when we understand that giving benefits the giver more than the receiver. "For it is in giving that we receive."

Jesus gave His life. Most of us are only expected to give some of our time or our talents or our treasures, which are all God-given. The Bible says that giving always leaves us with more, not less. "One man gives freely, yet gains even more; He who refreshes others will himself be refreshed" (Proverbs 11:25, NIV). "He who sows bountifully will also reap bountifully" (2 Corinthians 9:6, NASB).

> The Bible says that giving always leaves us with more, not less.

When it comes to giving, a few people always put themselves first; a few always put others first; all the rest of us fall somewhere in between. To grow in giving, every person needs to ask: Where do I fall on this continuum of giving? On those occasions when I'm able to put others first, the passage from Acts 20:35 (NASB) always rings true: "It is more blessed to give than to receive."

CHAPTER 8

FORGIVING

Forgiving is not the natural thing to do. There-fore, forgiving others for the hurt they inflict on us isn't easy. Human nature leans much more toward holding a grudge or seeking revenge. These are often accompanied with feelings of bitterness, hurt and anger. No matter how hard we resist, these emotions linger much longer than we would like. This condi-tion paralyzes us and causes discontent.

> Why not choose to ask God to prepare your heart on your journey to forgiveness toward others?

The good news is that God loves us in our strengths and our weaknesses. Total forgive-ness is there for all who place their trust and faith in Him, even when we fail. Extending forgiveness to those who have hurt us is necessary, if we are to experience God's forgiveness. Because God freely forgives us, we are asked to forgive others.

Why not choose to ask God to prepare your heart on your journey to forgiveness toward others? "Forgiveness allows us to live in peace with one another and with ourselves, which affords us the opportunity to step away from the hurt." — Miriam J. Stark

CHAPTER 9

THE LORD'S PRAYER

Prayer is an acknowledgment of our dependence upon God. It is the communion of the people of God with their heavenly Father. Prayer consists of praise, thanksgiving and confession. God's people present their prayers to God and leave it to Him to decide whether it is wise to grant the requests or not. God alone knows whether the content of the prayer would be for their own good or for the good of God's kingdom.

> God alone knows whether the content of the prayer would be for their own good or for the good of God's kingdom.

One day Jesus was praying in a certain place. When He finished, one of His disciples said to Him, "Lord, teach us to pray." Jesus responded with His teaching on prayer, which people later called **The Lord's Prayer**. He told them to pray the following (Luke 11:1-13, NIV):

Our Father in heaven hallowed be Your name. Just as very young children are totally dependent on their parents for survival, people of all ages stand to benefit from a similar relationship with their heavenly Father.

Your kingdom come. Your will be done on earth as it is in heaven. This refers to the heavenly, spiritual Kingdom of God to be established on earth at Christ's Second Coming to rule over all nations in the name of love.

Give us this day our daily bread. Bread represents the necessities of life, not the luxuries – our needs, not our wants. Montaigne wrote, "We are not to pray that all things may go on as we would have them, but as most conducing to the good of the world."

And forgive us our debts, as we forgive our debtors. There is a connection between the first and the second part of this petition. If you forgive others, you will be forgiven. We reap what we sow.

And do not lead us into temptation, but deliver us from the evil one. The request is for God's help in avoiding the array of worldly temptations; it will not be easy.

For Yours is the kingdom and the power and the glory forever. This refers to the Heavenly Kingdom of God that will be established on earth when Christ returns to rule over all nations with love, peace, joy and justice for all.

Amen. So be it.

The sixty-six words in this model prayer, as recorded in the sixth chapter of Matthew, serve as a guide for one's own personal prayer time.

CHAPTER 10
STRESS

Stress is the reaction of our bodies and minds to anything that upsets their regular balance. Doing the following will help reduce stress.

Accept yourself as you are. Don't try to be someone you aren't.

Accustom yourself to unreasonableness and injustice. Unfairness is common around us. Allow more time to get where you're going. It usually takes longer.

Always look on the positive side. It's the most constructive thing to do.

Be prepared to wait in line. Cultivate patience.

Concern yourself with the present. Tomorrow will take care of itself.

Deal with the little problems. It prevents big ones.

Discipline your children. Everyone will benefit from it.

Do the most important things first. And do them one at a time.

Exercise often. It does even more good than

most people realize.

Expect four out of five traffic lights to be red. Devote the time to prayer and introspection.

Focus on things as they are rather than how you want them to be.

Get outside of yourself. Help lighten the burdens of others.

Live within your means. Do everything possible to stay out of debt.

Schedule fewer activities. This allows time for the unforeseen.

Take care of yourself. That includes a balanced diet and eight hours of sleep.

> It's our perception of a situation that's at the root of much of the stress in our lives...

View trying circumstances as character-building opportunities. This results in the greatest good.

Watch less TV, especially "news" programs. TV is out to promote its own agenda.

We are not responsible for the actions of others. We can only change ourselves.

Write things down. Stop trying to remember everything.

It's our perception of a situation that's at the root of much of the stress in our lives, more than the actual circumstances. It's important for people to learn what they can do when confronted with stressful events because too much stress will cause physical and emotional damage.

CHAPTER 11

ACCOUNTABILITY

Individuals need to understand that God holds them responsible for what they are, for what they have been given, and for what they do with their gifts. That's accountability. "So then each of us shall give account of himself to God" (Romans 14:12, NKJV). "But I say to you that for every idle [careless] word men may speak, they will give account of it in the day of judgment" (Matthew 12:36, NKJV). Children do not have to try to look and be like everybody else, nor be something or someone they are not. God holds them accountable for what they are. No more, no less. "They will give an account to Him who is ready to judge the living and the dead" (1 Peter 4:5, NKJV). The Prophet Daniel put it this way: "The court was seated, and the books [which contain a complete record of everybody's life on earth] were opened"

Children will learn about accountability from you. This important task is not to be left to others.

(Daniel 7:10, NKJV).

Children will learn about accountability from you. This important task is not to be left to others. Children learn right from wrong early in life, but at times they may choose to do wrong anyway. Many think they can do what they want as long as nobody finds out. It should be made very clear to them that God knows their every work, thought, and deed before they do! "For there is nothing covered that will not be revealed, and hidden that will not be known" (Luke 12:2, NKJV).

CHAPTER 12

ANGER

Anger is good for you provided it's the right kind. The Bible talks about two kinds of anger: sinful and righteous. Sinful anger is excessive, uncontrolled rage whose intent is to punish and injure; that's not good. But righteous anger is controlled, thereby able to accomplish good. "Be angry and do not sin..." (Ephesians 4:26, NKJV). You can use anger with positive results. "Let no corrupt word proceed out of your mouth, but what is good for necessary edification [instruction] that it may impart grace to the hearers" (Ephesians 4:29, NKJV).

When children get angry, parents should first help them recognize it; second, admit it; third, take responsible action in dealing with it.

Hidden or denied anger may cause serious emotional and physical problems. Unresolved anger may surface in the form of headaches, stomach pains, ulcers, nail-biting, lying, cheating, rebellious school behavior, and high absenteeism, to mention a few. The sooner anger is confronted, the sooner it can be defused. "Do not let the sun go down on your wrath" (Ephesians 4:26, NKJV). Don't allow it to fester. Identifying the source of anger helps children avoid overreacting.

Children learn how to handle anger by observing their parents. God expresses His wisdom in the following passage: "He who is slow to wrath has great understanding, but he who is impulsive exalts folly" (Proverbs 14:29, NKJV). When children get angry, parents should first help them recognize it; second, admit it; and third, take responsible action in dealing with it. The best cure for anger is to do an unexpected kindness for the person he or she is angry at. This behavior will say, "I am sorry," better than any words.

CHAPTER 13

ATTITUDE

Attitude dictates our behavior. That's why it is so important to have a good one. "For as he thinks in his heart, so is he..." (Proverbs 23:7, NKJV). No matter the facts or circumstances, we have the choice and power to choose the attitude we take toward those facts and circumstances.

With children, attitude can be even more important than facts. Why? Because it depends on how they perceive the facts. Children with similar makeup and circumstances often see themselves differently. For example, some feel accepted while others feel rejected; some have high self-esteem while others feel unworthy; some feel appreciated while others do not; some see God as condemning while others see Him as loving, caring, and forgiving. Why?

> With children, attitude can be even more important than facts.

Parents need to be aware of how their attitudes affect their children. Children tend to adopt their parent's attitudes quite early in life. For example, when parents focus on the negative, children tend to do the same. But when parents look for the positive, children will learn that it is what is expected of them. The environment in which children are reared has so much to do with their attitudes about life.

CHAPTER 14

MONEY

Parents need to teach their children the value of money as early as possible. They should be allowed to make as many purchases with the money allotted them and live with mistakes and mismanagement—the price of learning. They should be encouraged to save some of their money to buy more expensive things later. They must learn to distinguish between needs and wants and practice the principle of using it up, making it do and wearing it out. It is never too early to encourage giving to charity and savings.

> Distinguish between needs and wants and practice the principle of using it up, making it do and wearing it out.

As they get older, encourage them to get a part-time job and open a savings account. As difficult as it may seem at times, the more parents persist, the more likely children will establish saving and spending habits that will last a lifetime.

CHAPTER 15
BUSY PEOPLE

Satan called a worldwide convention. In his opening address to his evil angels, he said, "We can't keep the Christians from going to church. We can't keep them from reading their Bibles and knowing the truth. We can't even keep them from forming an intimate, abiding relationship experience in Christ. If they gain that connection with Jesus, our power over them is broken.

"So let them go to their churches, let them have their conservative lifestyles, but steal their time, so they can't gain that relationship with Jesus Christ. This is what I want you to do, angels. Distract them from gaining hold of their Savior and maintaining that vital connection throughout their day!"

"How shall we do this?" shouted his angels.

> The evil angels went eagerly to their assignments causing Christians everywhere to get busy, busy, busy and to rush here and there.

"Keep them busy in the non-essentials of life and invent innumerable schemes to occupy their minds," he answered. "Tempt them to spend, spend and borrow, borrow, borrow. Persuade the wives to go to work for long hours and the husbands to work six to seven days a week, ten to twelve hours a day, so they can afford their empty lifestyles. Keep them from spending time with their children. As their family becomes fragmented, soon their home will offer no escape from the pressures of work!

"Over-stimulate their minds so that they cannot hear that still, small voice. Entice them to play the radio or cassette player whenever they drive and to keep the TV, VCR, CDs and their PCs going constantly in their homes. And see to it that every store and restaurant in the world plays non-Biblical music constantly. This will jam their minds and break that union with Christ.

"Fill the coffee table with magazines and newspapers. Pound their minds with the news twenty-four hours a day. Invade their driving moments with billboards. Flood their mailboxes with junk mail, mail-order catalogues, sweepstakes, services and false hopes. Keep skinny, beautiful models on the magazines so the husbands will believe that external beauty is what's important, and they'll become dissatisfied with their wives. Ha! That will fragment those families quickly!

"Even in their recreation, let them be excessive. Have them return from their recreation exhausted, disquieted and unprepared for the coming week. Don't let them go out in nature to reflect on God's wonders. Send them to amusements parks, sporting events, concerts and movies instead. Keep them busy, busy, busy! And when they meet for spiritual fellowship, involve them in gossip and small talk so that they leave with troubled consciences and unsettled emotions.

"Go ahead; let them be involved in soul-winning. But crowd their lives with so many good causes that they have no time to seek power from Christ. Soon they will be working in their own strength, sacrificing their health and family for the good of the cause. It will work! It will work!"

It was a quiet convention. And the evil angels went eagerly to their assignments causing Christians everywhere to get busy, busy, busy and to rush here and there.

I guess the question is, has the devil been successful at this scheme? You be the judge!

CHAPTER 16

CHARACTER

Character consists of a combination of emotional, intellectual and ethical traits that distinguishes one person (or group) from another. A person with good character is accountable, caring, fair, honest, kind, loving, sincere, trustworthy and more. If practicing these principles produces positive results (and it does), then the consequences of doing the opposite most surely will generate negative results.

Character is much easier to define than live out. At the risk of oversimplifying, building good character is simply a matter of teaching and practicing right from wrong and it doesn't happen over a short period of time. Nothing we could think, say or do comes even close to being as important as good character, and there is a devastating price to pay for underdeveloped character.

> Character development is the primary responsibility of parents.

So, when does character count? **Character counts in the home.** Character development is the primary responsibility of parents. If good character traits are not instilled in children early, often they are not learned at all. Here is where seeds of personal conduct and acceptable behavior are planted. Be responsible! Tell the truth! Respect your elders! Mind your manners! Treat others the way you want to be treated! And so on. Too often, parents place more emphasis on what children achieve rather than how they learn and interact with others. Good character development will not be quick and easy. It requires that children be closely supervised until maturity.

Character counts in school. Parents can no longer rely on the school system to teach good character as it once did. Character development is no longer a top priority. Culture has replaced it with its own version. Much behavior once considered inappropriate is now acceptable. Situational ethics now dominate and dictate what is considered proper behavior. Many absolute standards have become obsolete—a thing of the past. Adults and children alike need to take advantage of every opportunity to determine the differences between right and wrong and expect to pay the price when they deviate from these principles.

Character counts in the workplace. As valuable as knowledge of the job and training are, character is even more important. For example, traits that employers look for in their employees are honesty, dependability, reliability, punctuality, and the ability to get along with other employees by treating them the same way they want to be treated. Proper conduct does matter because it is the number one reason employees are not promoted or are fired.

Character counts in leadership. Look at the present generation and you see the character of our future leaders. Our national character is an accumulation of the principles and virtues practiced in our personal lives, homes, schools, workplaces, neighborhoods and positions of leadership, including the President of the United States. Leaders at all levels of society must set the example and serve as role models for future leaders. The character displayed by each citizen contributes to our national character for better or worse.

Character building is a continuous process. It is important to know that even small character flaws left unchecked can have seriously negative consequences. Good character traits must be an active force in the lives of everyone. When this is not the case, someone will get hurt. Every person alive is affected by the actions of others at some time, in some way, in some place.

An upright character is of greatest worth. It cannot be bought. The formation of a noble character is the work of a lifetime and can only be the result of diligent and persevering effort. Good character is what we look for in others and it is what others look for in us. So, when does character count? Character always counts.

CHAPTER 17

CHILDREN AND SCHOOL

By the time children are old enough to start school, they have come a long way and learned a great deal. They have done much of it on their own with parents as their teachers. Parents need to teach their children right from wrong and instill character traits, such as honesty, fairness, respect, honor, loyalty, kindness, dependability and manners.

Good students come to school ready to learn. Specifically, what does that mean? Good students do what's important:

> Few parents realize how much their children have learned by age six.

- pay attention, listen and concentrate
- follow classroom rules
- raise their hand before speaking
- participate and ask questions

Parents need to remind their children why school is important. They are there to learn to speak correctly, read, write, learn math, communicate, understand and be understood. Good students have specific goals, such as experiencing success, learning to be independent, and becoming law-abiding adults.

Few parents realize how much their children have learned by age six. They have become gender-conscious. They have acquired almost two-thirds of their height. They will be one-third of the way toward being practically on their own. Some child experts say that by six, children will have learned over half of their life-guiding principles for living, especially behavior-wise. Most of the seeds that influence behavior will have been planted. The kind of fruit they will bear, during the remaining school years and the rest of their lives, will result from these seeds.

Although many parents tend to blame the schools when their children don't do well, in reality, the schools are simply a reflection of the homes from which students come. They must accept the fact that it is they, and not the school, who are ultimately responsible for how their children turn out. They are the most important teachers their children will ever have. It is their example and caring that will be the major influence on attitude, accomplishments and behavior of their children.

Parents must realize that children differ in

their abilities and this will be reflected in their performance at different age levels. That is why it is so important for parents to get to know them individually. Children tend to do their best, even though at times it might not appear that way. Parents should avoid comparing their children with other children, especially brothers and sisters. It is best when children compete against themselves. By doing this, they can see their progress and find satisfaction in it. Children need to experience success or else they will give up and stop trying.

One of the areas that parents and educators need to examine more closely is the age at which children are permitted to start school. Attendance laws vary from state to state. Most school districts allow children to enroll as late as the September which falls closest to their sixth birthday (fifth for kindergarten). The assumption is that when children's birthdays fall in this range, they are all ready to start school physically, mentally and socially. Nothing could be further from reality.

Even children born on the same day differ. Children don't walk, talk, toilet train, or have the same interests at the same time. Therefore, it is unlikely that they would all be ready to do all that would be expected of them in school.

There are many possible reasons why performance varies among children. Differences are a major factor: age, intelligence, background, abilities, proper discipline, right attitude, and degree of maturity, especially the differences between girls, who tend to mature earlier, and boys, to mention a few.

When all these factors are taken into consideration—children who are younger because of birth date, children who differ in mental development, and the maturity differences between girls and boys—we are talking about a possible three-year age difference in the same classroom. Add to that the fact that they could be sitting next to each other.

Allowing children to start school before they are ready often leads to a continuous struggle of playing "catch up." In many instances, it may mean the difference between liking and hating school. In my experience as a teacher and guidance counselor for thirty-three years, I found that three out of four younger boys and one out of four younger girls encountered serious difficulties at school. The younger boys and girls who do succeed are usually above average in intelligence and come from above average home environments. Even in these cases, one can't help wondering whether they would have done even better with students their own age.

Age is not a perfect method to determine

when children should start school; however, it is unlikely to change in the near future. My recommendation is that children who turn six in June or later of that year (five for kindergarten) would be wise to wait until September of the following year to enroll. This means that all first-graders will then turn seven (six for kindergarteners) by the end of the school year. Whereas now, the June, July, August and September birthdays (one-third of first-graders and one-third of kindergarteners) respectively are still six and five by the end of the school year. It is to the student's advantage to be one of the older rather than younger members of the class, especially boys.

There are other long-term consequences and considerations. Many children younger than their classmates tend to struggle in school and end up with a poor self-image. If immaturity is the problem, the gap will widen more each year and achievement will continue to drop off. When children can't or don't keep up, they often will be teased about it. Poor school performance becomes a constant source of bickering and frustration at home and in school. Grade levels dictate expectations forcing students into social situations before they are really ready such as sports, dances, proms, dating, and other social activities. When younger students go out for sports, they must compete against older classmates. Younger students may be at a disadvantage when taking college entrance and scholarship tests and managing on their own away from home. Later is better!

CHAPTER 18
CONSEQUENCES

Consequences are the results of actions taken by people based on their definition of right and wrong. The differences are beyond one's imagination. On the one hand are those who say, "Treat me the way I want to be treated." Everyone else falls somewhere between these two extremes: Who's right? Who's wrong?

Although many people disagree with the numerous aspects of what's right and what's wrong, they do agree that society could not survive without laws that define some form of right from wrong behavior. Obviously, this is why laws that conform to accepted standards of right and wrong, and have endured the test of time, have been established and put in place.

Negative behavior produces negative consequences. Positive behavior produces positive consequences. We reap what we sow. It can't be any other way! The time span between the actions and the consequences will often vary. In fact, it's possible that they may not become known in one's lifetime. But one thing is certain: someone, sometime, somewhere will inherit the consequences.

To what degree people abide by civil and moral laws will determine whether the consequences of their actions will be positive or negative. The following character traits are just a sampling of the hundreds of moral principles and guidelines by which people live: abusive, anxious, envious, generous, grateful, greedy, honest, kind, loving, patient, promiscuous, and successful. Readers are encouraged to analyze and determine what effects they might have in their lives and then apply these insights to the many other facets of their lives. What determines which road you travel on your journey of life? What is your moral compass?

> Negative behavior produces negative consequences. Positive behavior produces positive consequences. We reap what we sow.

Everyone subscribes to some kind of guiding force or god to determine what's right or wrong for them: atheism, fame, humanism, money, popularity, power, secularism, success, witchcraft, to name a few. What one chooses to value most becomes his or her god.

Just as following natural laws such as gravity protects us from physical harm, obeying civil and moral laws shield us from much of life's needless suffering. This makes it more possible for us to live more meaningful, constructive and productive lives.

CHAPTER 19

DEATH: HEAVEN OR HELL?

Death is the most certain thing in life and often prepared for the least. The soul is that part of one's being that is thought of as who we really are. It continues after physical death and leaves the body intact to eternal life in Heaven (paradise) or Hell (torment). God makes this judgment based on the only thing that accompanies us—our character—not on the inventory that we leave behind.

"There shall be a resurrection of the dead, both of the just and unjust" (Acts 24:15, KJV). This is Biblical truth. One may choose not to believe it, but that doesn't make it any less true.

What happens to people after they die? Everyone must answer this question for himself or herself and their children when they ask. The Bible's answer is clear beyond doubt. Those who believe and trust in Jesus as their Lord and Savior will spend eternity with Him in Heaven. Non-believers, those who choose a different path will spend eternity separated from Him in Hell. It is one or the other. People are free to believe or not believe and live and die with the consequences of that choice. I agree with those who think a measure of Heaven and Hell is experienced while we are still living on this earth.

On what basis do people make the greatest decision they will ever make? The Bible teaches that there are two kinds of birth: physical birth, which we have nothing to do with, and spiritual birth, which we have every-

Those who believe and trust in Jesus as their Lord and Savior will spend eternity with Him in Heaven.

thing to do with. "Unless one is born again [the second birth] he [she] cannot experience the Kingdom of God. That which is born of the flesh is flesh, and that which is born of the Spirit is spirit" (John 3:3, KJV).The flesh dies, but the spirit lives in eternity.

The second birth is not something that we inherit from our parents. It's a choice and decision that each person must make for himself or herself, when they feel called to do so. The rebirth experience is a gradual unfolding process that continues throughout life, much like babies mature into adulthood. Then God opens their eyes to a different lifestyle with new meaning and purpose. Their way of living will develop in the direction that their spiritual birth leads them. They will become more God-centered and less self-centered, learning to do more of what is right in God's sight.

Salvation is our greatest need. Why? Because we are all born with a sinful nature. Because of this, we are hostile and antagonistic toward God. We want to do it our way instead of God's way. The end result is sin. Sin is the act of disobeying God's laws, intentionally or unintentionally. It's worth noting that often we are not punished for our sins but rather, because of their consequences.

So, what's the solution? To the believer, God's word in the book of Romans (NASB) equips us with a simple, clear and foolproof plan: Admit you are a sinner. "For all have sinned and come short of the glory of God" (3:23). Believe that Jesus Christ died for your sins. "But God demonstrates His love toward us, in that, while we were yet sinners, Christ died for us" (5:8). Commit your life to Jesus. "For whosoever shall call upon the name of the Lord shall be saved" (10:13).

CHAPTER 20
DENOMINATIONALISM

Denominations are religious groups that have much in common and assemble for worship. They may refer to themselves as an assembly, congregation, or by a specified church name, such as those noted below, none of which appear in the Bible.

The Cleveland phone book lists over 100 denominations and 200 independent churches.

Today in America seventy-five percent of adults identify themselves as Christian. In comparison, the next largest religions in America are Islam and Judaism. Combined they represent only one to two percent of the USA population. However, there are more than 1,500 different Christian faiths in America. (Which one is right?)

Christianity is ranked as the largest religion in the world today with approximately 2 billion adherents. Thirty-three percent of the world's population is considered to be Christian, and there are approximately 38,000 Christian denominations. This statistic takes into consideration cultural distinctions of denominations in different countries. The Roman Catholic Church is the largest Christian group today with more than a billion followers constituting about half of the world's population. (Reference: *World Christian Encyclopedia*).

Denominations differ on a variety of issues, including Biblical interpretation, customs and traditions; social issues of birth control, abortion and homosexuality, clergy, heaven, hell and purgatory, sacraments (baptism, communion, etc.), saints, sinners and salvation (faith alone or good works, spiritual second birth), tithing (gross, net), and when and how to worship.

> The closer an individual, group or church parallels the Bible, the better equipped they will be to distinguish right from wrong.

In the last 2,000 years, Christianity has gone from one Christian denomination (The Church of God, the only church name recorded in the Bible) to more than 1,500 different denominations and cults. Could the following be some negative consequences from this evolution: a decrease in church attendance (about one in three attend church services), over half of all marriages end in divorce, half of all babies are born out of wedlock, a weakening of the family, and a decline in moral values? One could conclude that denominations with closer attention to Biblical principles would be a major step in the right direction.

No church is perfect because all of its members (no matter the hierarchy) are imperfect due to man's sinful nature. All violate God's laws to one degree or another. It's time for members of all denominations to focus on what they have in common, rather than on their differences, and learn from one another. The closer an individual, group or church parallels the Bible, the better equipped they will be to distinguish right from wrong. Mark Twain, who didn't consider himself religious, said, "Some people claim they are troubled by parts of the Bible which they cannot understand. What troubles me is that part of the Bible which I understand only too well."

Jesus summarized the total Bible message very simply: "Love the Lord your God with all your **heart** and with all your **soul** and with all your **mind**. This is the first and greatest commandment. And the second is like it. Love your neighbor as yourself" (Matthew 22:37-39, NIV). Let's try to keep it simple and find common ground.

CHAPTER 21

DILIGENCE

Faith is the root of the Christian way of life. It requires nourishment, and one of the main nutrients to nourish faith is diligence. In fact, it demands it! Diligence means to proceed in one's undertaking in a careful, steady, persistent and understanding way. In the words of writer Henry M. Morris, Ph.D., each person is commanded to "be diligent in diligence."

On what do we focus our diligence? Seven guiding principles that will help produce a well-rounded, fruitful Christian life are recorded in the Bible in 2 Peter 1. They are designed to nurture our faith in God's word and include the following:

> Diligence means to proceed in one's undertaking in a careful, steady, persistent and understanding way.

- Virtue (goodness, justice, moral, excellence)
- Knowledge (comprehension, Scripture, understanding)
- Temperance (abstinence, moderation,

perseverance)
• Patience (calmness, endurance, steadfastness)
• Godliness (devotion, holiness, reverence)
• Brotherly Kindness (friendship, mercy, tolerance)
• Charity (affection, Christian love, forgiveness)

The above listing, as important as it is, is far from exhaustive. It goes without saying that to what degree people practice these principles will vary from person to person in accordance with his or her age, maturity level and giftedness. Fortunately, salvation becomes a reality by belief and faith in Christ as our personal Savior, by grace not our works.

By way of illustration and encouragement, visualize yourself as a newborn baby and how, with loving care, proper support and steadfast patience, adulthood becomes a reality. This same scenario is just as applicable to the Christian way of life.

Practicing the above principles to the best of one's ability should influence an individual's attitudes, actions and relationships in a positive direction. The Bible encourages us to "love each other deeply, because love covers over a multitude of sins" (1 Peter 4:8, NIV).

CHAPTER 22

EDUCATION

There is much concern today about the negative trends in education in America: decline in education in America, decline in educational standards, drop in standardized achievement test scores, severe discipline problems, unexcused tardiness and absences, vandalism, theft, cheating, lying, drug abuses and promiscuity to mention a few.

In a November 2010 speech, Secretary of Education Arne Duncan reported that "one-quarter of U.S. high school students drop out or fail to graduate on time. Almost one million students leave our schools for the street each year."

About this same time, a group of top retired generals and admirals released the following information, stated by Arne Duncan: "Seventy-five percent of young Americans, between the ages of 17 to 24, are unable to enlist in the military today because they have failed to graduate from high school, have a criminal record, or are physically unfit. America's youth are now tied for ninth in the world in college attainment" ("Does America

Have a Future?" *Sunday Book Review*, David Frum, September 8, 2011).

Duncan has initiated several reforms to achieve the highest educational standards. His biggest push is to raise the status of the teaching profession. Why?

Tony Wagner, the Harvard-based education expert and author of *The Global Achievement Gap*, explains it this way: "There are three basic skills that students need if they want to thrive in a knowledge economy: the ability to do critical thinking and problem-solving, the ability to communicate effectively, and the ability to collaborate."

Parents who rear their children by God's laws can rest assured that they will serve them throughout their lives.

Two of the countries that lead in these skills are Finland and Denmark. They insist that their teachers come from the top one-third of their college graduating class. As Wagner put it, "They took teaching from an assembly-line job to a knowledge-worker's job. They have invested massively in how they recruit, train and support teachers, to attract and retain the best."

I certainly agree that the recruitment of teachers needs to be upgraded. After devoting thirty-three years to the educational system of America as a teacher and counselor, I'm of the opinion that one-fourth of the teachers do an excellent job, one-half do an adequate job, and one-fourth do a poor job.

Thomas L. Friedman, columnist for The New York Times, in an article titled "Teaching for America" is in total agreement with Duncan and Wagner and adds "all good ideas, but if we want better teachers, we also need better parents—parents who turn off the television and video games, make sure homework is completed, encourage reading and elevate learning as the most important life skill. The more we demand from teachers, the more we have to demand from students and parents. That's the contract for America that will truly ensure our national security."

I would add another skill to those of Duncan, Wagner and Friedman: moral principles that spell out right and wrong behavior. Ethics is the process by which these determinations are made; for the Godly, the process is always God-centered rather than self-centered where anything goes.

Children need moral standards to make the right behavioral choices. Godly principles provide and equip them with those standards. Parents who rear their children by God's laws can rest assured that they will serve them throughout their lives.

God holds parents responsible for teaching their children right and wrong. Teaching moral principles is an ongoing process, and that is why it's so important for parents to be with their children as much as possible, especially during the formative years.

In children's eyes, their parents are god. So, before parents can teach their children about the one true God they want them to follow, they must make sure that they are representing Him accurately in their own lives. Chances are children are going to worship the god of their parents, whoever or whatever it is.

CHAPTER 23

JOURNEY

What determines which road you travel on your journey of life? What guidelines do you follow to navigate your own personal life and that of your children, and what influences how you conduct yourself with other people? What is your moral compass?

Everyone subscribes to someone, something or some kind of god or gods (philosophy) to determine what's right and what's wrong for them: academics, atheism, capitalism, communism, humanism, money, polytheism (many gods), power, popularity, narcissism, various religions, secularism, success and witchcraft, to name a few. What one serves is his or her "god."

Do you really know the right way to live? Our culture would have us believe that each individual is the ultimate authority of what's right and what's wrong, rather than following what has been proven to be right in the past. If someone you trust informs you that something is poisonous, for example, wouldn't it make sense to investigate it first before using it in some way?

Just as following natural laws protects us from physical harm, following moral laws shields us from much of life's needless suffering and permits us to live meaningful lives. People require and need sound standards to make good moral choices.

Following moral laws shields us from much of life's needless suffering and permits us to live meaningful lives.

In order to achieve this, after a lifetime of contemplation, inquiry and comparison, my personal choice is The Holy Bible, specifically the Ten Commandments. These have proven to be the best way for me to determine right from wrong. In my opinion, they are applicable to everyone.

These laws need to be brought to the attention of as many people as possible, but not forced on anyone, except those involving murder, libel and theft. Situations require that each person thinks and decides which moral compass he or she chooses to follow.

CHAPTER 24
LIVING THE MOMENT

On what does your mind focus most of the time? When people are asked this question, the most frequent response is on the future, then the past, and lastly the present. This is unfortunate because the present is the most critical and where the action is.

Think about driving a car! Now and then we look back via the rear-view mirror. Occasionally, we look ahead to approaching areas. But mostly, we need to focus on the immediate present in order to arrive at our destination. This illustration applies to living life as well.

Only after we begin to look back on our lives do we realize how much time, effort and worry we devoted to things, situations and circumstances that were and are out of our hands. These can be little matters when we are young and/or bigger matters when we are older.

Any area of concern over which we have no control is cause for worry and becomes a "no win" situation that detracts us from where we can and do make a difference. Only after we begin to identify and dismiss those things that are out of our hands are we in a position to focus our time and effort on the here-and-now in bringing about constructive and positive changes. This results in less worry, greater accomplishments and improved quality of life for the individual and those with whom he or she comes in contact.

Consider the following viewpoint. "First, I was dying to finish high school and start college. And then I was dying to finish college and start working. And then I was dying to marry and have children. And then I was dying for my children to grow old enough so I could return to work. And then I was dying to retire. And now, I am dying...and suddenly I realize I forgot to live."

> There are two days in every week about which we should not worry—two days which should be kept free from fear and apprehension.

There are two days in every week about which we should not worry—two days which should be kept free from fear and apprehension. One of those days is yesterday. Learn from its mistakes, fault, blunders, aches and pains, and put it away. The other day we should not worry about is tomorrow with its possible adversities, burdens and promises. This leaves only one day—**today**. Anyone can fight the battle of just one day. It is only when we add the burdens of yesterday and tomorrow that we break down.

In the words of writer Kay Lyons Stockham, "Yesterday is a cancelled check, tomorrow is a promissory note; today is the only cash we have—so spend it wisely."

CHAPTER 25

LOVE

The word love means different things to different people. The Reverend Harry Wendt defines four different kinds of love. He writes the following:

The word "love" is sometimes confused with the word "like." Perhaps that is because the English language has only one word, "love," to explain a number of ideas. The Greek language, however, uses a number of terms:

Eros: Eros acts in response to an attraction in another person; it usually involves physical or sexual appeal. It is also an act of the emotions and cannot be commanded.

Philia: Has to do with companionship. It has often been called the "friendship" type of love.

> God's love is unconditional and people, especially children, need unconditional love.

Storge (store-gay): Refers to love between family members.

Agape (ah-gah-pay): This love acts in response

to a need in another person. It is an act of the will, and **can** be commanded. This word is used to describe God's love for mankind and the love people are to have for one another in response.

"Love is patient, love is kind. It does not envy, it does not boast, it is not proud. It does not dishonor others; it is not self-seeking, it is not easily angered, it keeps no record of wrongs. Love does not delight in evil but rejoices with the truth. It always protects, always trusts, always hopes, always perseveres.

"Love never fails. But where there are prophecies, they will cease; where there are tongues, they will be stilled; where there is knowledge, it will pass away" (1 Corinthians 13:4-8, NIV).

God's love is unconditional and people, especially children, need unconditional love. They need to be loved if they are to grow up to be loving. They need love, security, and acceptance from the very beginning. They need praise, encouragement, and instruction more than correction, even when they are not very loving.

CHAPTER 26

MARRIAGE

Children learn about marriage from their parents. This begins very early in life. They use their parents' marriage as a model. This is what they take with them to their marriage and pass on to their children. They should be exposed to the struggles as well as the successes. Their expectations need to be realistic. Somehow the message that marriage is not all fun and games doesn't get through. They need to know that all households have their share of sadness and joy. Parents should not hesitate to discuss these matters at the appropriate time. Many opportunities to do this will arise naturally, such as at mealtimes, weddings, funerals, reunions and hundreds of other occasions. Discussing the Christian marriage with children helps prepare them for the event in their own lives.

In the beginning, God established the marriage bond. "Have you not read that He who made them at the beginning made them male and female," and said, "For this reason a man shall leave his father and mother and be joined to his wife, and the two shall become one flesh?" (Matthew 19:4-6, NASB). Marriage is the most intimate relationship and it was designed to be one of the most fulfilling and rewarding. For this to be true, however, Biblical principles pertaining to marriage must be followed. "Unless the Lord builds the house, they labor in vain who build it..." (Psalm 127:4, NASB). Marriage is not a human invention; it is God's creation.

For marriage to be what God intended, He has to be at the center. My way and your way are replaced with His way, looking upward rather than inward. "Submitting to one another in the fear [reverence] of God" (Ephesians 5:21, NKJV). Mutually submitting to one another and to God means husbands and wives are able to consider the needs of the other as more important than their own. To do this, they keep God at the center of their marriage and submit to His teachings. When their fragile support lines intertwine with Him, they form an unbreakable cord. "And a threefold cord is not quickly broken" (Ecclesiastes 4:12, NKJV). Since all husbands and wives are imperfect, they should not expect perfection in their marriage. Only God is perfect. This is why with God at the center of

> Marriage is not a human invention; it is God's creation.

the marriage, all things become manageable.

One of the most important factors in marriage is choosing the right partner. The Bible is very specific about this. "Do not be unequally yoked together with unbelievers..." (2 Corinthians 6:14, NKJV). Unequally yoked means the marriage will be built using two different sets of blueprints. Being equally yoked means using the same set of blueprints to build the marriage. Neither will be built without hard work. But which one is likely to encounter more problems? The most important ingredient of a good and happy Christian marriage is that husband and wife share a common faith and belief in God. Though this doesn't guarantee a good marriage, couples who do not share a common faith are more likely to experience difficulties in marriage. Children need to be made aware of this information even though they may choose to ignore it when they select their marriage partner.

Children also need to be aware of the differences between husbands and wives. God meant each of them to be unique. Though they differ physically, mentally, emotionally, and may have different gifts they are all of equal value and importance in God's eyes. God didn't put all strength of character on one sex. The differing masculine and feminine gifts and talents are to be mutually respected and appreciated. They are intended to complement, not battle against each other. This understanding is not only essential for a good marriage, but also it provides a solid sex identity model for healthy childrearing by doing such things as the following: trying to see the other's point of view; resolving conflicts as soon as possible; being as forgiving as possible; asking what he or she can do to help; trying to maintain a prayerful attitude; learning to be the person God wants him or her to be; avoiding blame because it only makes matters worse; and treating each other as he or she would want to be treated.

Remember, it's important that you serve as a good role model for your children. They'll be watching!

CHAPTER 27

PARADOX

The paradox of our time in history is that we have taller buildings, but shorter tempers; wider freeways, but narrower viewpoints; we spend more, but have less; we buy more, but enjoy it less.

We have bigger houses and small families; more conveniences, but less time; we have more degrees, but less sense; more knowledge, but less judgment; more experts, but more problems; more medicine, but less wellness.

We drink too much, smoke too much, spend too much, laugh too little, drive too fast, get angry too quickly, stay up too late, get up too tired, read too seldom, watch TV too much, and pray too seldom.

We've done larger things, but not better things.

We have multiplied our possessions, but reduced our values. We talk too much, love too seldom, and hate too often. We've learned how to make a living, but not a life; we've added years to our life, not life to years.

We've been all the way to the moon and back, but have trouble crossing the street to meet the new neighbor. We've conquered outer space, but not inner space. We've done larger things, but not better things.

We've cleaned up the air, but polluted the soul. We've split the atom, but not our prejudice. We write more, but learn less; we plan more, but accomplish less.

We've learned to rush, but not to wait; we have higher incomes, but lower morals; we have more food, but less appeasement; we build more computers to hold more information to produce more copies than ever, but have less communication; we've become long on quantity, but short on quality.

These are the times of fast food and slow digestion; tall men, and short characters; steep profits, and shallow relationships.

CHAPTER 28

PRAYER

Perhaps nothing on the subject of prayer has ever been uttered more wisely than the following speech in the Constitutional Convention of 1787. The speaker was in his 82nd year:

"In the beginning of the contest with Britain, when we were sensible of danger, we had daily prayer in this room for the Divine Protection. Our prayers, Sir, were heard, and they were graciously answered. All of us who were engaged in the struggle must have observed frequent instances of superintending providence in our favor. To that kind providence we owe this happy opportunity of consulting in peace on the means of establishing our future national felicity.

> If a sparrow cannot fall to the ground without His notice, is it probable that an empire can rise without his aid?

"And have we now forgotten this powerful Friend? Or do we imagine we no longer need His assistance. I have lived, Sir, for a long time; and the longer I live, the more convincing proofs I see of this truth—that God governs in the affairs of men. And if a sparrow cannot fall to the ground without His notice, is it probable that an empire can rise without his aid?

"We have been assured, Sir, in the Sacred Writings, that 'except the Lord build the house, they labor in vain that build it' (Psalm 127:1, KJV).

"I firmly believe this; and I also believe that without his concurring aid we shall succeed in this political building no better than the builders of Babel: we ourselves shall be divided by our little, partial local interests; our prospects will be confounded, and we ourselves shall become a reproach and a by-word down to future age.

"And what is worse, mankind may hereafter from this unfortunate instance, despair of establishing governments by human wisdom, and leave it to chance, war, or conquest. I therefore, beg leave to move that henceforth prayers imploring the assistance of Heaven and its blessing on our deliberations, be held in this assembly every morning before we proceed to business, and that one or more of the clergy of this city be requested to officiate in that service."

—Benjamin Franklin

CHAPTER 29
RELATIONSHIPS

Relationships are connections between people, places, and things and how they relate to one another. They can be voluntary or involuntary, positive or negative, constructive or destructive.

There are good relationships but no perfect ones because there are no perfect people. The challenge is to nurture the best relationships possible with family members, friends and co-workers.

I want to focus here on people relationships that are voluntary, positive and constructive. What are the ingredients of such relationships? What follows is my attempt to answer this question.

> Avoiding the negative aspects of conduct is a great enhancement to building meaningful relationships.

Six guiding principles establishing healthy relationships appear in the Bible in the fourth chapter of Philippians, where we are encouraged to meditate on any virtue and anything praise-worthy, including the following: whatever things are true (accurate, factual, genuine), noble (honorable, sincere, trustworthy), just (honest, impartial, lawful), pure (moral, sinless, uncorrupted), lovely (enjoyable, loving, pleasing), and of good report (beneficial, prudent, suitable).

Avoiding the negative aspects of conduct is a great enhancement to building meaningful relationships. In Ephesians 4:31-32 (NKJV) we read, "Let all bitterness, wrath, anger, clamor, and evil speaking be put away from you, with all malice. And be kind to one another, tenderhearted, forgiving one another, even as God in Christ forgave you."

Should we not adhere to this instruction, we not only hurt ourselves and others, but we displease God.

As important as it is to have a loving relationship with people, it is even more critical that every individual experience a personal relationship with the God of Scripture. Better to have a personal relationship with Him than to attend church and not have it. Of course, having it and attending church would be even more beneficial.

Cultivating voluntary, positive constructive personal relationships helps make the impossible possible. Life is all about relationships.

CHAPTER 30

SUCCESS

Success: What is it? Webster defines it as the result that was hoped for: the fact of becoming rich, famous, etc. Generally speaking, success falls in either one of two categories: Godly, the God-centered way of love toward God and love toward others, and worldly, the self-centered way of greed and unconcern for the welfare of others. We are required to make choices, like it or not. We can't have it both ways.

Most people who seek success choose the route of becoming rich and famous. Theologian Herbert W. Armstrong writes about just such people: "Their definition of success was material acquisition, recognition of status by society, and the passing enjoyment of the five senses. But the more they acquired, the more they wanted, and the less satisfied they became with what they had. When they got it, it was never enough." A prime example of this is King Solomon, who was called

> All who have succeeded have followed these seven laws of success.

the wisest and wealthiest man who ever lived. He had it all and concluded at the end of his life, "It was all vanity and a striving after wind" (Ecclesiastes 1:14, ESV).

"Why are only the very few—women as well as men—successful in life?" asks Armstrong, "Just what is success?" Here is the surprising answer to life's most difficult problem, providing that no human need ever become a failure! All who have succeeded have followed these seven laws of success:

1. Fix the right goal. The very first law of success is to be able to define success! Once you have learned what success is, make that your goal in life.

2. Education or preparation. We have to learn, to study, to be educated, and to be prepared for what we propose to do. Right education must not stop at teaching to live! It must know and teach the purpose of human life and how to fulfill it.

3. Health. We are physical beings and are what we eat. Of course, there are other laws of health: sufficient sleep, exercise, plenty of fresh air, cleanliness and proper elimination, right thinking, clean living.

4. Drive. Half-hearted effort might carry one a little way toward his goal. But it will never get him far enough to reach it. Without energy, drive, and constant propulsion, a person need never expect to become truly successful

5. Resourcefulness. When complications, obstacles, unexpected circumstances appear to block your path, you must be equipped with resourcefulness to solve the problem, overcome the obstacle, and continue on your course.

6. Perseverance,   stick-to-it-iveness. Nine out of ten people, at least once or twice in a lifetime, come to the place where they appear to be totally defeated! All is lost—apparently, that is. They give up and quit, when just a little more determined hanging on, just a little more faith and perseverance, just a little more stick-to-it-iveness would have turned apparent certain failure into glorious success.

7. God. This all-important Law of Success is having contact with, and the guidance and continuous help, of God. And the person who does put it last is very probably dooming his life to failure at the end.

"The only way to success is not a copyrighted formula being sold for a price. You can't buy it! The price is your own application to the seven existing laws." —Herbert W. Armstrong

What do you think? Do you agree? Do you disagree?

CHAPTER 31

TELEVISION

Television is one of the greatest inventions of all time. Since the 1950s, it has affected people's lives more than any other technological development. For the first time in history, something other than parents has become the main provider of information, values and entertainment for children. TV has changed how the family functions, how people think, what they buy, how they dress, and what they do during their free time.

Surveys tell us that average pre-school-age children, age two to five, spend a third or more of their total waking hours watching TV. Most children will spend more time watching TV than any other single activity during the first 18 years of their lives except sleep.

> Most children will spend more time watching TV than any other single activity during the first 18 years of their lives except sleep.

Television can be a great blessing. At its best it can inform, expand and enrich the lives of adults and children, but it can also be a curse. It can rob adults and children of their moral and spiritual values and cripple their mental, emotional and physical development. The wrong use of television can do the following: cause confusion between right and wrong, retard social development, make learning in school more difficult, shorten attention span, reduce attentiveness, discourage self-discipline, harm parent-child relationships, interfere with mealtime, increase boredom, promote spectatorship rather than participation, rob time from reading, writing, conversing, playing, exercising and imagining, and mislead children into believing difficult problems can be easily solved in a short period of time.

Parents are responsible for preventing television from ruling their family. They should not assume that TV is always acceptable entertainment. In fact, the opposite is true. TV programming is saturated with violence, sex, distorted role models, trivia and immorality.

CHAPTER 32

PRESENT

In our culture, all of us are preoccupied most of the time with anticipating the future and worrying about it or with daydreaming about the past and remembering how it was. We are always trying to be happier right now, and yet much of what we do prevents us from achieving that happiness.

To be in the here and now means to be in touch with our senses, to be aware of what we are seeing, hearing, smelling, and so on. Young children find it very easy to be in the here and now. If we watch them play, we will notice that they seldom worry about what is going to happen an hour or two hours from now, and they spend little time reminiscing. They are concerned with the present situation and with getting the most from it.

> If, as teenagers and adults, we could be more like young children, many of the problems that bother us would disappear.

If, as teenagers and adults, we could be more

97

like young children, many of the problems that bother us would disappear.

Think about how many nights we were not able to get to sleep because we were thinking about the future or the past; how many hours of the day we wasted and how many opportunities we have missed by not allowing our mind and body to experience what is happening now.

CHAPTER 33

ROOM

In that place between wakefulness and dreams, I found myself in the room. There were no distinguishing features except for one wall covered with small index card files. They were the ones in libraries that list titles by author or subject in alphabetical order. But these files, which stretched from floor to ceiling and seemingly endlessly in either direction, had very different headings.

As I drew near the wall of files, the first to catch my attention was one that read, "People I have liked." I opened it and began flipping through the cards.

I quickly shut it, shocked to realize that I recognized the names written on each one.

And then without being told, I knew exactly where I was. This lifeless room, with its small files, was a crude catalog system for my life. Here were written the actions of my every moment, big and small, in a detail my memory couldn't match.

A sense of wonder and curiosity, souled with horror, stirred within me as I began randomly opening files and exploring their content. Some brought joy and sweet memories; others a sense of shame and regret so intense that I would look over my shoulder to see if anyone was watching. A file named "Friends" was next to one marked "Friends I Have Betrayed."

The titles ranged from the mundane to the outright weird. "Books I Have Read," "Lies I Have Told," "Comfort I Have Given," "Jokes I Have Laughed At." Some were almost hilarious in their exactness: "Things I've Yelled at My Brothers." Others I couldn't laugh at: "Things I have Done in my Anger," "Things I have Muttered Under My Breath at My Parents." I never ceased to be surprised by the contents. Often there were many more cards than I expected. Sometimes, fewer than I hoped.

But then as I pushed away the tears, I saw Him.

I was overwhelmed by the sheer volume of the life I had lived. Could it be possible that I had the time in my short life to write each of these thousands or even millions of cards? But each card confirmed this truth. Each was written in my own handwriting. Each signed with my own signature.

When I came to a file marked "Lustful Thoughts," I felt a chill run through my body. I pulled the file out only an inch, not willing to test its size, and drew out a card. I shuddered at its detailed content. I felt sick to think that such a moment had been recorded.

An almost animal rage broke in me. One thought dominated my mind: No one must ever see these cards! No one must ever see this room. I have to destroy them. In an insane frenzy, I yanked the file out. Its size didn't matter now. I had to empty it and burn the cards.

But as I took it at one end and began pounding it on the floor, I could not dislodge a single card. I became desperate and pulled out a card, only to find it as strong as steel when I tried to tear it.

Defeated and utterly helpless, I returned the file to its slot. Leaning my forehead against the wall, I let out a long, self-pitying sigh. And then I saw it. The title bore "People I have Shared the Gospel With." The handle was brighter than those around it, newer, almost unused. I pulled on its handle and a small box not more than three inches long fell into my hands. I could count the cards it contained on one hand.

And then the tears came. I began to weep sobs so deeply that the hurt started in my stomach and shook through me. I fell on my knees and cried. I cried out of shame from the overwhelming humiliation of it all. The rows of file shelves swirled in my tear-filled eyes. No one must ever, ever know of this room. I must lock it up and hide the key.

But then as I pushed away the tears, I saw

Him. No, please not Him. Not here. Oh, anyone but Jesus. I watched helplessly as He began to open the files and read the cards. I couldn't bear to watch His response. And in the moment when I could bring myself to look at His face, I saw a sorrow deeper than my own. He seemed to intuitively go to the worst boxes. Why did He have to read every one?

Finally He turned and looked at me from across the room. He looked at me with pity in His eyes. But this was a pity that didn't anger me. I dropped my head, covered my face with my hands and began to cry again. He walked over and put His arm around me. He could have said so many things. But He didn't say a word. He just cried with me.

Then He got up and walked back to the wall of files. Starting at one end of the room, He took out a file and, one by one, began to sign His name over mine on each card.

"No!" I shouted rushing to Him. All I could find to say was, "No, no," as I pulled the card from Him. His name shouldn't be on these cards. But there it was, written in red so rich, so dark, so alive. The name of Jesus covered mine. It was written with His blood.

He gently took the card back. He smiled a sad smile and began to sign the cards. I don't think I'll ever understand how He did it so quickly, but the next instant it seemed I heard Him close the last file and walk back to my side. He placed His hand on my shoulder and said, "It is finished."I stood up, and He led me out of the room. There was no lock on its door. There were still cards to be written.

—Joshua Harris, "The Room"

CHAPTER 34
TRUTH

There are all kinds of truth out there. As someone so aptly put it, "There are three truths: my truth, your truth and THE truth." The definition of truth as used here is God's word, the Bible, the pillar and foundation of belief in absolute truth, where hundreds of references speak words of truth, always in love.

Godly truth is determined by God's word (God-centered), the Ten Commandments in particular. Worldly truth (self-centered) is determined by the culture. All truth is relevant; Bible truth never changes—it is the same "yesterday and today and forever." Worldly truth is the opposite; it is in constant change. Nothing is absolute; anything goes. Whenever these differences are ignored, negative consequences are sure to follow.

"The Parable of the Sower" is a short, simple, worldly story that teaches godly truth. Jesus said, "A farmer went out to sow his seed. As he was scattering the seed, some fell along the path; it was trampled on, and the birds of the air ate it up. Some fell on rock, and when it came up, the plants withered because they had no moisture. Other seed fell among thorns, which grew up with it and choked the plants. Still other seed fell on good soil. It came up and yielded a crop a hundred times more than was sown."

In Luke 8:9-15 (NIV), Jesus' disciples asked him what this parable meant. "This is the meaning of the parable: Those along the path are the ones who hear, and then the devil comes and takes away the word from their hearts, so that they may not believe and be saved. Those on the rock are the ones who receive the word with joy when they hear it, but they have no root. They believe for a while, but in the time of testing, they fall away. The seed that fell among thorns stands for those who hear, but as they go on their way they are choked by life's worries, riches, and pleasures and they do not mature. But the seed on good soil stands for those with a noble and good heart, who hear the word, retain it, and by preserving, produce a crop." Which soil best describes you? Does this parable imply that only one out of four people can be counted on to tell the truth and abide in God's word?

> Do not be disloyal toward others by withholding or distorting the truth with intent to deceive.

The ninth commandment says, "You shall not give false testimony." Do not be disloyal toward others by withholding or distorting the truth with intent to deceive. Remember, God loves every person equally. In the words of J. Grant Howard, "Truth is not limited to the Scriptures, but it is limited by the Scriptures." When it comes to what is really true, we must admit that certain truths never change. If it is true, it's true, whether people believe it or not. Truths are timeless. They provide guidance when making tough decisions. They add meaning and give purpose to life. They have served us well in the past. The more people stray from Biblical principles, the more disheartening the present and future will become.

"To love our neighbor as ourselves is such a truth for regulating human society, that by that alone one might determine all cases in social morality."

—John Locke

CHAPTER 35

IDENTITY

What makes us the way we are? First, our heredity, the passing on of certain characteristics from parents to offspring, the genes we inherit at conception. Second, our environment: all the things, conditions and influences that surround us, both positive and negative, especially during the early, pre-school years. Third, parental health care.

In *Origins: How the Nine Months Before Birth Shape the Rest of Our Lives,* author Annie Murphy Paul writes the following: "Much of what a pregnant woman encounters in her daily life—the air she breathes, the food and drink she consumes, the chemicals she's exposed to, even the emotions she feels—is shared in some fashion with her fetus." She continues noting that these factors shape a person as a baby and a child and continue to have an effect throughout life.

Children respond to their environment based

> One of the most important gifts a parent can give a child is the gift of that child's uniqueness.

to a great extent on their inherited characteristics. However, they should not be made to feel inferior or cheated because of hereditary differences. They have no control over it. They can't change it. And their worth as a human being should not depend on it. It's God's plan for them to be different. Therefore, they should not be compared to one another. When parents view their children in this light, they not only prevent them from feeling inferior or superior, but they actually help them discover God's plan for their lives.

"One of the most important gifts a parent can give a child is the gift of that child's uniqueness... Children's parents are the very best people to let them know that they are different, that there are no others in the whole world who are exactly like them, and that their differences are part of what makes them special and lovable. When parents value their child's uniqueness, that child can learn self-worth and the worth of others as well."

—Fred Rogers

CHAPTER 36
WORRY

Parents should encourage children to trust God in all things, "Trust in the Lord with all your heart, and lean not on your own understanding" (Proverbs 3:5-6, NIV). This kind of wisdom takes the worry out of living. Throughout life, children will encounter situations they can do nothing about. These must be accepted as part of God's divine plan. They need to focus on those situations they can do something about. Children have to move in the direction of taking on more and more responsibility for their actions. God has given them a mind and He expects them to use it. Children need to learn to take charge of their lives and not have it the other way around.

> Parents should help their children avoid the worry habit. It's acquired.

Parents should help their children avoid the worry habit. It's acquired. We aren't born with it. It's destructive. Doctors tell us that worry by far is the greatest cause of illness. Symptoms of excessive worry in children include nail biting, hair pulling, overeating, digestive problems, elimination difficulties, depression and many more. Not only does worry hurt children emotionally and physically, but also it undermines their faith and trust in God, which compounds the problem even more.

God doesn't want anybody to be a slave to worry. "Be anxious for nothing, but in everything by prayer and supplication, with thanksgiving, let your requests be made known to God, and the peace of God which surpasses all understanding, will guard your hearts and minds through Christ Jesus" (Philippians 4:6-8, NASB). When children come to the understanding that everything that worries them can be placed under God's control, His word will lead them to peace, joy and confidence.

Parents have to help children sort through the things they worry about. This means separating those things they can do something about from those they can't. They will soon learn that most things people worry about never happen. And those that do aren't nearly as bad as imagined. This will allow them to focus on the present and deal with matters that require their attention. "This is the day the Lord has made; we will rejoice and be glad in it" (Psalm 118:24, NKJV).

Worriers can become so occupied with the past and future that the present gets ignored. Living is not unlike driving a car. Occasionally, the driver should look back and far ahead. But mostly, they should look at the road immediately in front of them. When children learn from yesterday and concentrate on today, tomorrow usually takes care of itself.

Children worry most when they experience fear and anxiety that their needs will not be met. Simply telling them not to worry doesn't get the job done. Little children are totally dependent on their parents. They trust them and expect them to be wise in looking out for their welfare.

When children's needs are met, worry will have a hard time taking root.

CHAPTER 37

JESUS

The moral and spiritual values born out of His Word provide the foundation for sound character and good citizenship. Jesus reveals Himself in the following "I AM" statements as recorded in John's gospel:

"I AM the bread of life. He who comes to me shall never hunger, and he who believes in me shall never thirst."

"I AM the light of the world. He who follows me shall not walk in darkness, but have the light of life."

"I AM the door. If anyone enters by me, he will be saved."

"I AM the good shepherd. The good shepherd gives his life for the sheep."

"I AM the resurrection and the life. He who believes in me, though he may die, he shall live."

> I AM the way, the truth, and the life. No one comes to the Father except through me.

"I AM the way, the truth, and the life. No one comes to the Father except through me."

"I AM the vine; you are the branches. He who abides in me, and I in him, bears much fruit; for without me you can do nothing."

Use what you need, but don't deny others through waste. "If anyone has material possessions and sees a brother or sister in need but has no pity on them, how can the love of God be in him?" (1 John 3:17, NIV).

"All we like sheep have gone astray; we have turned, every one, to his own way" (Isaiah 53:6, NKJV).

CHAPTER 38

GROWING

Lord, Thou knowest better than I that I am growing older and will someday be old. Keep me from the fatal habits of thinking I must say something on every subject and on every occasion. Release me from craving to straighten out everybody's affairs. Make me thoughtful, but not moody; helpful, but not bossy. With my vast store of wisdom, it seems a pity not to use it all; but Thou knowest, Lord, that I want a few friends at the end. Keep my mind free from the recital of endless details; give me wings to get to the point. Seal my lips on my aches and pains; they are increasing and love of rehearsing them is becoming sweeter as the years go by. I dare not ask for improved memory, but for a growing humility, and a lessening cocksureness when my memory seems to clash with the memories or others. Teach me the glorious lesson that occasionally I may be

> Give the ability to see good things in unexpected places and talents in unexpected people.

mistaken. Keep me reasonably sweet, for a sour old person is one of the crowning works of the devil. Give the ability to see good things in unexpected places and talents in unexpected people, and give, O Lord, the grace to tell them so. Amen.

—Attributed to Mother Teresa

CHAPTER 49

BOOM

In 2006, for the first time in American history, more than half of babies born to women younger than 30, 50.4 percent, were born to unwed mothers. That should give Americans pause because of the poverty and other harmful consequences associated with single parenthood. Some single mothers, especially those closer to thirty, will encounter more hurdles than their married counterparts, but they are more likely to succeed, if they've earned a college degree and have a good job and a strong support network. But younger women who are alone and not prepared for motherhood face huge problems with significant implications for their children and the public that must support families that can't support themselves.

> Having children without two parents is a recipe for poverty.

Having children without two parents is a recipe for poverty. Young, single mothers face enormous challenges in getting the education needed to launch a career. Many don't graduate from high school. Even more don't go to college, and if they do, they don't graduate. Lifetime earnings potential is severely reduced without a degree.

Many of these struggling single-parent families don't pay taxes; about 40% are below or near the poverty level and need public assistance. Each family headed by a woman who hasn't graduated from high school costs the public about $7,000 a year to support.

Society is not going to return to the 1950s and traditional male and female roles, but it still needs ethics about the responsibilities of making and raising babies (The Plain Dealer Cleveland, September 21, 2008).

The negative consequences not noted in this editorial are endless: sexual disease, regrets, guilt, abortion, child abuse, to mention a few. Unwed mothers can't even begin to imagine what lies ahead. What values will they pass on to their children? God's word does not detail the impact of illicit sex, but it does say that it is wrong.

CHAPTER 40

JUDGING

People who judge others often do it to make themselves look better at the expense of others. God says to hate the sin but love the sinner, regardless of the nature of the sin. It's to be left to God to separate right from wrong. He "will render to each one according to his deeds" (Romans 2:6, NKJV). "For by your words you will be justified, and by your words you will be condemned" (Matthew 12:37, NKJV). He will do this in His own time. All have sinned. All come short of the glory of God. None achieves perfection in this life.

When the scribes and Pharisees pressed Jesus to pass judgment on the woman taken in adultery, Jesus responded in the following way: "'He who is without sin among you, let him throw a stone at her first.' When Jesus had

> When children give other children the opportunity to learn, grow, and change rather than condemn, they themselves benefit as well as others.

121

raised Himself up and saw no one but the woman He said to her, 'Woman, where are those accusers of yours? Has no one condemned you?' She said, 'No one, Lord.' And Jesus said to her, 'Neither do I condemn you; go and sin no more'" (John 8:7-14, NKJV).

When children give other children the opportunity to learn, grow, and change rather than condemn, they themselves benefit as well as others. "Judge not, and you shall not be judged. Condemn not, and you shall not be condemned. Forgive, and you will be forgiven" (Luke 6:37, NKJV). Children need to understand that their rewards and punishment, in this life and the life after, will be based on their conduct and performance in this life.

CHAPTER 41

PATIENCE

Patience is the ability to calmly endure unpleasant situations. Exercising self-control under trying circumstances presents the greatest challenge of all. "Count it all joy when you fall into various trials, knowing that the testing of your faith produces patience" (James 1:2-4, NKJV). Being patient means looking beyond present circumstances. We are to dwell on the fact that God is in charge rather than set our minds on complaining.

Parents should do everything possible to cultivate patience in their children. The reason it's so important is that impatience is the cause of most unhappiness. Patience should be encouraged when children's wants, needs, and goals are not met immediately. They need to be reminded that each minute, hour, and day that passes brings them closer to the end result.

> Patience promotes peace of mind, good health, and more importantly, glorifies God.

Children should be reminded that their problems during their lives on earth represent a moment in time compared to eternity. "Do not forget this one thing that with the Lord one day is like a thousand years, and a thousand years as one day" (2 Peter 3:8, NKJV). "And let us not grow weary while doing good, for in due season we shall reap if we do not lose heart" (Galatians 6:9, NKJV).

Patient people make the most of their trying times. They maintain a positive outlook. They seek to improve the situation. They think of ways to use the waiting time profitably.

Patience promotes peace of mind, good health, and more importantly, glorifies God. Parents need to make every effort possible to instruct their children in the Godly trait of patience.

CHAPTER 42

PROCRASTINATION

Procrastination is needless delay. It is weakness in our character that prevents us from doing what needs to be done. Often, it's something people choose to avoid or escape from because it's distasteful. They tell themselves they'll do it later. Laziness is also part of the problem. Procrastination is a sinful human failing that only a few escape totally.

Parents do anything they can to minimize procrastination in their later years. The most unfortunate thing about this habit is all the time that is wasted. Over time, it robs children of their self-respect, mental health, new opportunities, and time that could be devoted to many other useful activities.

> Procrastination is a sinful human failing that only a few escape totally.

Overcoming procrastination is not easy. It leaves a trail of unfinished business wherever it goes. Attempts to justify it include making excuses, apologies, and regrets. People who accomplish much good in their lives can serve as inspiration. They have dealt with the problem and this is what allows them to get so much done. Impressing upon children the importance of time is a good place to begin.

Certain opportunities may occur only once in a lifetime. If they are not seized at that point, they may be lost forever. The odds of this happening with the procrastinator are much greater. Children need to be reminded of God's expectations of them.

CHAPTER 43

BIRTH

At some point, all adults as well as children, must, of their own free will, decide to accept Jesus as their personal Savior. The spiritual will then follow. Jesus says, "Unless one is born of water and the Spirit, he cannot enter the kingdom of God. That which is born of the flesh is flesh, and that which is born of the Spirit is spirit" (John 3:5-6, NKJV). The flesh dies, but the Spirit lives in eternity.

It's important for parents to know that most people who come to know Christ do so before they are old enough to leave home. Parents should do all they can to influence a spiritual birth, but they can't do it all. Jesus says, "No one can come to Me unless the Father who sent Me draws him..." (John 6:44, NKJV). The rebirth experience is a gradual unfolding process that continues throughout life, much like a baby grows into adulthood. Children are not born from

> The rebirth experience is a gradual unfolding process that continues throughout life.

above again because their parents are. They must experience this for themselves. Then God opens their eyes to a life with new meaning and purpose.

Children need to be taught they will never understand everything there is to know about God. "No one can find out the work that God does from the beginning to end," (Ecclesiastes 3:11, NKJV). It is like each generation painting part of a painting, but no one sees the painting completed. This is the way God intended it to be, but by learning about God in His Holy Word and trusting in His promises, He will become such a power in their lives they will soon learn to do what is right in His sight.

CHAPTER 44

TEMPTATION

Temptation is anything that lures or entices us to act outside of God's will. It's not a sin to be tempted, but it is sinful to yield to it. "Let no one say when he is tempted, 'I am tempted of God'; for God cannot be tempted by evil, nor does He Himself tempt anyone. But each one is tempted when he is drawn away by his own desires and enticed. Then when desire has conceived it gives birth to sin; and sin, when it is full-grown, brings forth death" (James 1:13-14, NKJV).

When children find themselves tempted to act outside God's will, parents should encourage them to ask, what would happen if I yielded? Would it be worth the consequences? They should be honest in thinking through the outcome. Ask God for strength to resist temptation. "Watch and pray,

> When children find themselves tempted to act outside God's will, parents should encourage them to ask, what would happen if I yielded?

lest you enter into temptation. The spirit indeed is willing, but the flesh is weak" (Matthew 26:41, NKJV).

"No temptation has overtaken you except such as is common to man; but God is faithful, who will not allow you to be tempted beyond what you are able, but with the temptation will also make the way of escape, that you may be able to bear it" (1 Corinthians 10:13-18, NKJV). "Blessed is the man who endures temptation; for when he has been approved, he will receive the crown of life which the Lord has promised to those who love Him" (James 1:12, NKJV). By trusting in what God says is right and doing what God would have them do, children can be assured that God's grace will be there to help them resist temptation where and when they need it.

CHAPTER 45

TRUTHFULNESS

Truthfulness is a character trait that needs to be instilled very early in children. They will face many opportunities when they will be tempted to avoid or turn from the truth because of the cost involved. It's important they decide in advance how they will react when such occasions arise. They may find it hard to do at first, but such experiences help them stand for what is right when there's pressure from their peers to compromise their integrity.

Parents, by example, can best teach their children the principles of truthfulness. It is at this junction in their young lives that they decide which fork in the road they will take, the road of God's truth or the road of self-truth. "Therefore, putting away lying, 'let each of you speak truth with his neighbor', for we are members of one another" (Ephesians 4:25, NKJV). "Buy the truth, and do not sell it, also wisdom and instruction and understanding" (Proverbs 23:23,

> Acquired truth allows God to be in charge of our lives.

NKJV). "God our Savior desires all men to be saved and to come to the knowledge of the truth" (1 Timothy 2:4, NKJV). This acquired truth allows God to be in charge of our lives.

One of God's most exciting promises is found in John's gospel where Jesus said, "If you abide in My work, you are My disciples indeed. And you shall know the truth and the truth shall make you free" (John 8:31-32, NKJV). Freedom from the weaknesses of human nature. Freedom from thoughts, words, and actions that hurt and destroy self and others. Freedom from earthly sin that leads to eternal death. This acquired freedom allows God to direct our lives so we can reap His many blessings.

CHAPTER 46

WORLDLINESS

The Scripture has much to say about worldliness. Following is a selection of those passages; Jesus said we are to be mindful of the things of God not of the world. "For what will it profit a man if he gains the whole world and loses his soul...?" (Mark 8:36, NKJV). "Do you not know that friendship with the world is enmity with God? Whoever therefore wants to be a friend of the world makes himself an enemy of God" (James 4:4, NKJV). "For where your treasure is, there your heart will be also" (Matthew 6:21, NKJV).

Children need to be taught that the only thing they can count on with certainty in this world is God because everything else is constantly changing.

> Jesus teaches that materialism apart from God leads to destruction.

Jesus teaches that materialism apart from God leads to destruction. Most people, in many ways, live opposite of what God intended. They will need to prepare for the fact that as Christians, they will face opposition and criticism. God-fearing people have always been and will continue to be in the minority.

Children need to be taught what it means for them to be in the world but not of it. They need to understand that God's standards should influence the world and not the other way around. "Set your mind on things above, not on things on earth" (Colossians 3:2, NKJV). "He who loves his life [puts God second] will lose it, and he who hates his life [puts God first] in this world will keep it for eternal life" (John 12:25, NKJV).

"Let your conduct be without covetousness; be content with such things as you have" (Hebrews 13:5, NKJV). Children are to strive for behavior that pleases God.

CHAPTER 47

WALKING

At some point early in our lives, we begin to investigate our small world by crawling. As we get older, stronger, and wiser, we expand our world by learning to walk. In time, these first faltering baby steps, accomplished with many falls and bruises, lead into the steady strides that carry us through a lifetime of purposeful activities.

God expects from us what a healthy parent expects of a toddler learning to walk. He recognizes that our first steps along the path of belief will be like those of the infant trying his legs for the first time. Only with time and through His grace and nurturing are we able to turn those first unsteady toddler's steps into giant leaps of faith.

> As children of God, we spend our lives learning to walk in the path of His Son, Jesus.

When you embark on a new path of faith, start with baby steps. Develop your inner strength and confidence through the tumbles and bruises that are a necessary part of growth. Make a commitment through daily prayer to get up after each fall and proceed with courage and dedication toward your goal. As children of God, we spend our lives learning to walk in the path of His Son, Jesus. Remember that He is with you and shares your excitement as you follow in His footsteps to overcome the hurdles and bars of life.

CHAPTER 48

RESURRECTION

Parents need to inform their children about God's promises about eternal life. "But I do not want you to be ignorant, brethren, concerning those who have fallen asleep, lest you sorrow as others who have no hope. For if we believe that Jesus died and rose again, even so God will bring with Him those who sleep in Jesus. For this we say to you by the word of the Lord, that we who are alive and remain until the coming of the Lord will by no means precede those who are asleep. For the Lord Himself will descend from heaven with a shout, with the voice of an archangel, and with the trumpet of God. And the dead in Christ will rise first. Then we who are alive and remain shall be caught up together with them in the clouds to meet the Lord in the air. And thus, we shall always be with the Lord. Therefore

> Parents need to see that their children know about and understand what the resurrection means for them.

comfort one another with these words" (1 Thessalonians 4:13, NKJV).

Children should know that their loved ones who have died in the faith will continue to live and that they, too, who are alive in Christ, will live and that all people who live and die in Christ will live.

The day will come when each one of us will have to give account of our lives. Parents need to see that their children know about and understand what the resurrection means for them. Jesus said "I am the resurrection and the life. He who believes in Me though he may die, he shall live" (John 11:25, NKJV). This knowledge and understanding of the resurrection places our own death and the death of our loved ones and others in the proper perspective. There is much about the afterlife that God has chosen not to reveal to us. But this one is perfectly clear: all believers will live in eternity with Christ.

BIBLIOGRAPHY

Armstrong, Herbert. *The Seven Laws of Success.* Philadelphia Church of God, 2013.

Duncan, Arne. Interviewed by Christiane Amanpour on ABC's "This Week with Christiane Amanpour", August 29, 2010.

Eidenmuller, Michael. *Great Speeches for Better Speaking*, Ben Franklin quoted from his address on prayer at the Constitutional Convention. McGraw Hill, 2008.

Friedman, Thomas L. *Teaching for America*, The New York Times, November 20, 2010.

Gibbon, Edward. *The Decline and Fall of the Roman Empire.* London: Strahan & Cadell, 1776.

Harris, Joshua. New Attitude Magazine, 1995.

Howard, J. Grant. quoted in *Changing Hearts by Changing Minds*, GraspingGod.com, 2012.

Lewis, C.S. *Mere Christianity.* HarperCollins Publishers, 1952.

Locke, John. *John Locke Quotes.* BrainyQuote.com, BrainyMedia Inc, 2019. https://www.brainyquote.com/quotes/john_locke_151487

Morris, Henry. *Days of Praise.* Institute of Creation Research, 2007.

Niebuhr, Reinhold. *Serenity Prayer.* First published in A Book of Prayers and Services for the Armed

Forces, 1944.

Paul, Annie Murphy. *How the Nine Months Before Birth Shape the Rest of Our Lives*, New York: Free Press, a Division of Simon & Schuster, 2010.

Rogers, Fred. *Fred Rogers Quotes*. BrainyQuote. com, BrainyMedia Inc, 2019. https://www. brainyquote.com/quotes/fred_rogers_947887.

Wagner, Tony. *The Global Achievement Gap*. New York: Basic Books, 2008.

World Christian Encyclopedia, Edinburgh University Press.

KEYS TO AN AMAZING LIFE: EVERYDAY WISDOM FOR YOUR SUCCESS

IF YOU'RE A FAN OF THIS BOOK, WILL YOU HELP ME SPREAD THE WORD?

• There are several ways you can help me get the word out about the message of this book…

• Post a 5-Star review on Amazon.

• Write about the book on your Facebook, Twitter, Instagram – any social media you regularly use!

• If you blog, consider referencing the book, or publishing an excerpt from the book with a link back to the Amazon page. You have my permission to do this as long as you provide proper credit.

• Recommend the book to friends – word-of-mouth is still the most effective form of advertising.

• Purchase additional copies to give away as gifts.

Enjoy these Other Books by Dan Taddeo

I BELIEVE...A UNIQUE COLLECTION OF TRUTH, WISDOM AND COMMON SENSE

I Believe provides insight to help you find peace, comfort, under-standing, direction, even solutions to the challenges and opportunities life brings.

WORDS OF WISDOM, TOO: A TREASURY OF INSPIRATIONAL MESSAGES FOR YOUR CONTEMPLATION.

A powerful collection of life-transforming messages from throughout the ages. The selections have appealed to people over years as praiseworthy thoughts that are instrumental in the development of the American Character.

SCRIPTURE SERVINGS FOR SPIRITUAL STRENGTH

Scripture Servings....is a unique daily devotional because it contains no commentary or application save the conviction of the Scriptures themselves upon the heart of the reader. With over 260 relevant topics containing more than 2,700 biblical passages spread out over 366 pages, you will find plenty to nourish your daily appetite.

COURSE OF ACTION: MOTIVATION, INSPIRATION, AND DIRECTION TO ENHANCE YOUR LIFE

Here is a unique selection of essays and notable quotables. These concise and relevant topics are guaranteed to fertilize and cultivate your life and challenge you to become more involved in focusing on the true meaning of life.

BACK TO BASICS: PARENTING PRINCIPLES, A BIBLICAL PERSPECTIVE

Parenting is a tremendous challenge in our complex world. This book offers suggestions for raising children in an age of relaxed moral standards and single-parent homes.

ONE NATION WITHOUT GOD: FACING THE CONSEQUENCES OF A SOCIETY THAT NO LONGER VALUES CHOOSING RIGHT FROM WRONG

History is filled with great civilizations that have come and gone. They all experienced moral decay from within. This book documents the cultural and moral changes that have brought devastating consequences upon our society in the last two generations.

THE CONTROVERSY: GODLINESS VS. WORLDLINESS

No one can serve two masters. This book contains a selection of inspirational writings featuring a broad variety of subjects pertaining to life. It is an anthology of eight previously published books.

NOTABLE QUOTABLES: 3,000 QUOTATIONS FROM A TO Z

Captured within this volume are nuggets of wisdom from Thomas Jefferson, Mother Theresa, Martin Luther King, Jr., John F. Kennedy,

Margaret Mitchell, Winston Churchill, Golda Meir and countless others-pertaining to topics from A to Z.

You can order these books from

or wherever you purchase your favorite books.